Feelings and other things

AF624532

Cassandra Byl

BookLeaf Publishing

Presentation by *BookLeaf Publishing*

Web: www.bookleafpub.com

E-mail: info@bookleafpub.com

ISBN: 9789357211642

First edition 2023

Roses are red

Roses are red,
Violets are blue.
It's what they always said,
But let me tell you,
Roses come in many colours
This I know is true.

Roses are red.

Roses are red
Violets are blue,
I like you,
Do you like me too?

Daisies and Carnations

Daisies are yellow
Carnations are pink.
You're a nice person
Should we date do you think?

Love

When a man loves a woman,
He provides for her and protects her.
When a woman loves a man,
She tries not to poison him with her cooking.

Confidence

Confidence is hard to hold onto,
But very easy to lose.

Mans best friend.

Always their for me
No matter the day or the time
My dearest friend
The keeper of my secrets.
All that is asked of me in return
A little food, shelter, time and love.
She is my beautiful best friend
She is my dog.

This place

The Best place in the world to be,
Right here, right now.

The grass is greener.

Wherever grass is fed and watered
This is where the grass is always greener.

Myself

I stood at the bottom of the drive
Waiving goodbye to my life.
Tomorrow things were going to be different
Everything was changing
Because I was choosing myself.

Breathe deep

Overcome your fear and anxiety
For they are not real.
Do not breathe life into them.
Close your eyes
Breathe in deeply
Feel your strength and your courage
Breathe in deeply once again
Feel your light and your happiness
Create beauty from within
The masterpiece of all that you are
And now
Breathe deeply

Jump in

Standing on the edge of the cliff
Almost ready to jump
The water below crystal clear
Then I feel the thumping in my body
Fear kicking in, to keep me safe
But it makes my legs weak, they buckle under me
I stumble and fall into the blue waters below
It's cold but I am safe, and that was fun
Next thing you know.
I'm standing on the cliff.

Beautiful

Be all you can
Easily and honestly
Aspire to do great things
Understanding is needed
Totally fine to take a breath
Invite your higher self
Fullfill your wishes
Unapologetically be 100% yourself
Love laughter and light.

Mirror

Mirror mirror on the wall
Who is the luckiest girl of all?
Why that's easy it's you dear one.

Take a bow

You deserve a standing ovation
For all you have endured
This journey called life is trying
But you haven't let it beat you
Yes it may knock you down from time to time
But you dear girl always get back up and keep trying
So you deserve a standing ovation
So stand up beautiful and take a bow.

She is

She is a gypsy
Free in her travel
Never feeling the need to stay put in one place.
She is a mermaid
Riding the waves of life as they come,
And sometimes seeking solitude for a moment on the oceans floor
She is a hippie
With love for the land and all creatures on it
Carrying peace in her heart
She is all of these, and so so much more.

Today, Tomorrow, Yesterday

We have tomorrow before us
It's just a day away
But don't look towards it yet
For you need to live today.
Yesterday has been and gone
It came and went so fast
Don't sit thinking about that to long as that's now in the past
Live today be present make every minute count
For soon enough the tides will turn and the days will change about.

Nothing to hide

Do not hide your truth
Not for any reason
For to hide is to deceive
Do not deceive yourself no matter what
You are the most important person in your life
So stop holding back
Stop hiding and stop pretending
For there is no reason to do so
Show who you really are
Show that bold honest courageous soul
That is inside of you
Let her out, give her a voice let her take the stage
Now then their you are
I see you I feel you
You are safe you are loved
And there is nothing to hide

Unclipped the unleashing of within

Today I unclip myself from your reigns
Today I set myself free and you in the process
You go your way and I'll go mine.
I will no longer listen to your criticism or your judgement
I am no longer feeling hurt by you
No more sufferings no more sadness
And no more questioning
Unleashed
I'll go my way and you go yours.

www.ingramcontent.com/pod-product-compliance
Lightning Source LLC
Chambersburg PA
CBHW051723130826
49812CB00034B/1321
9789357211642

bloom little flower

Irene Limon

BookLeaf Publishing

Presentation by *BookLeaf Publishing*

Web: www.bookleafpub.com

E-mail: info@bookleafpub.com

ISBN: 9789357442718

First edition 2023

Dedicated to my loving husband Joseph, my two beautiful children Aurora and Rowan. I cherish every moment with you!

bloom little flower

be still little one,
stay safe in my arms.
now reach for the sun,
avoid every harm.
bloom like no one is watching!

Earth

soil solidified,
quiet clashing Titans rise,
all is still again.

She is solid ground,
our Mother in life and death,
all return some day.

Water

forever dancing,
playful, harsh, unforgiving
eternal movement.

fluid, in motion
constant channels move our world,
wash away my pain.

Air

rush past, Silent One
always there but never Seen.
secrets/ screams alike.

soft caress, my heart
feels you there, a shadow near
whispers, "always mine"

Fire

sparks, colors Ignite
engulf thy passions in Red
She consumes, then kills.

slick quick licks become
fast raging pain, Destruction
a new world of ashes.

singing bee

tell me your sticky secrets,
sing them to me Bee.
drip like honey,
hum them, thoughts
in a floral melody.
please will you sing them
sweetly little Bee.

Human

being Human is kind of like...
Love, sweet tenderness
cuddles, dreams & kisses.
squishy Feelings
melted together with complication.
something missing in between
each laugh, each hug, each other.
Curiosity, endless like stars
asking, begging to be Seen.
Shining bright,
a slow burn builds.
Colliding realities
create more... Love.
Human.

roots

Deep, deep, deep
deep down.
Solid connection
Flowing toxicity
through veins of love.
Love to give,
love to take,
love to hurt,
love to hate...
These roots are mine
not mine alone.
Ours.
Past loves, past lives, past mistakes
always there.
Through years
twisted, entangled,
deep deep down,
inside.

little deaths

dormant soul, darkness
infinite slumber, alive
Reborn, flesh & wild

Cosmic Gift

the gift of universal love,
equivalent to eternal pain
naive affections present
deep hollow hearts.
a child born of heartache,
fill the void.
glare into the sun,
let flames singe reality.
explode ecstasy to the mass,
nothing but stardust...

balance

cruelty & kindness
harmony in symmetry
our Euphoric bliss

water me please

I see you
sitting there.
My muse, delicate
Sweet and beautiful.
Slowly, you droop
you gravitate closer
Downward.
I see you
but forget to show you the
Love and compassion you deserve.
If only you could
Reach out and
Seize all that you desire.

soar high

Hurry! catch a gust
wind stirs in a flurry, go!
take the plunge, soar High

flor

Fiery petals
dance & sway with the soft breeze
Vibrant energy

exotic in flow
erotic kiss to lips, skin
Blush of color, mine

when the sun sets

when the sun sets on us
please don't cry.
don't tell me all the reasons why
it's all my fault
I didn't try
to light your sky
forever.
what I need is time
when all rivers of love run dry
time to heal time to grow
please don't pry
when the sun sets on us...

Welcome

life on Earth is bittersweet,
lots of work and tons to eat.
No one knows just what to say,
so they set out to spend the day
trying to make things better.
we all try not to start a fight
to help keep all we're feeling light.
if you're new here, that's okay
we all stumble and lose our way
just take a breathe...
try happy

whispers of moon

Lying on the ground at night
Starting straight up at the sky
I hear a voice.
Softly it caresses flesh
Slips into mind, fearless.
Echoes of wisdom trickle through
Gravitating towards the heart
I feel it.
Whispers of moon
Guiding, trying to be heard
Healing, crying, praying
For you.
She sings a sweet song
Powerful and true
That you may someday too
Whisper songs of love to the moon.

forget me not

when my petals fall away
and she takes beauty
recall each laugh & smile shared...

(forget me not)

find me in the clouds

if you're ever looking
find me in the clouds
high in the sky
where birds sing sweetly
floating along the
wondrous colors
blending dream with reality.

www.ingramcontent.com/pod-product-compliance
Lightning Source LLC
Chambersburg PA
CBHW051723130826
49812CB00034B/1320
9789357442718